dick bruna

I can count

Tate Publishing

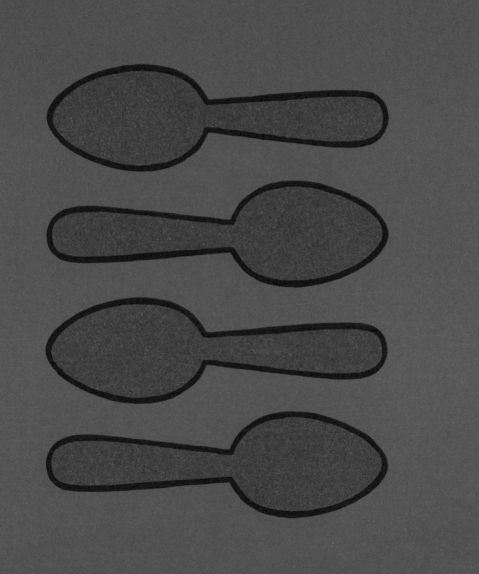

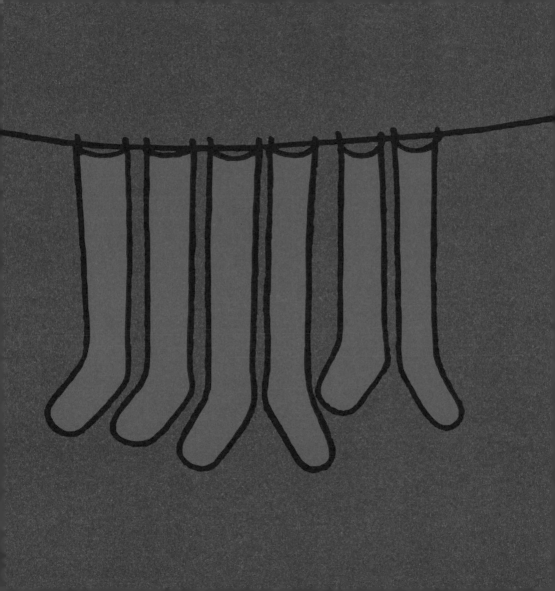

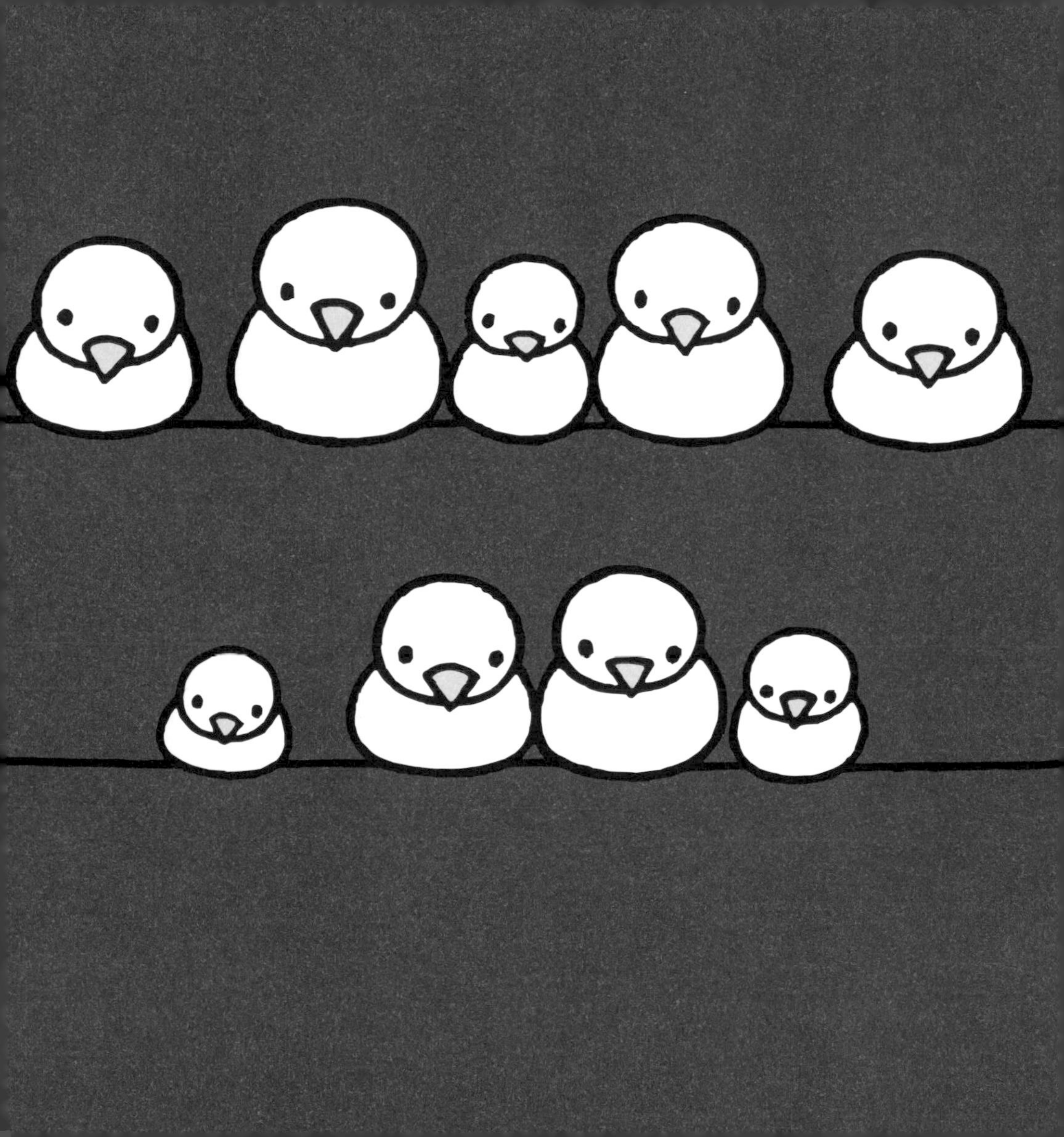

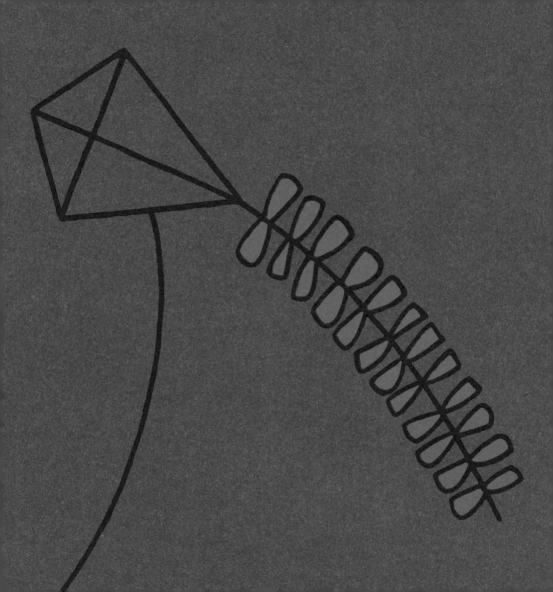

Other Dick Bruna books available from Tate Publishing:

round, square, triangle 2012
miffy the artist 2008
my vest is white 2012

Published 2012 by order of the Tate Trustees
by Tate Publishing, a division of Tate Enterprises Ltd,
Millbank, London SW1P 4RG
www.tate.org.uk/publishing

This edition © Tate 2012. Reprinted 2012.

Original edition: *telboek*
Original text Dick Bruna © copyright Mercis Publishing bv, 1968
Illustrations Dick Bruna © copyright Mercis bv, 1968
Publication licensed by Mercis Publishing bv, Amsterdam
Printed by Sachsendruck Plauen GmbH, Germany
All rights reserved.

A catalogue record for this book is available from the British Library
ISBN 978 1 84976 076 8
Distributed in the United States and Canada by ABRAMS, New York
Library of Congress Control Number: applied for